W0099545

Foods

Contents

 Look and put the sticker.

juice

jelly

cookies

pizza

Sticker

 Put sticker on the word.

Do you like juice ?

Yes, I do.

 Ask and say.

Color and say.

 Sticker

 cookies

fish

apples

cookies

pizza

bread

juice

 pizza

juice

cookies

jelly

pizza

ice cream

 Look and put the sticker.

fish

bread

ice cream

apples

 **Put sticker on the word.**

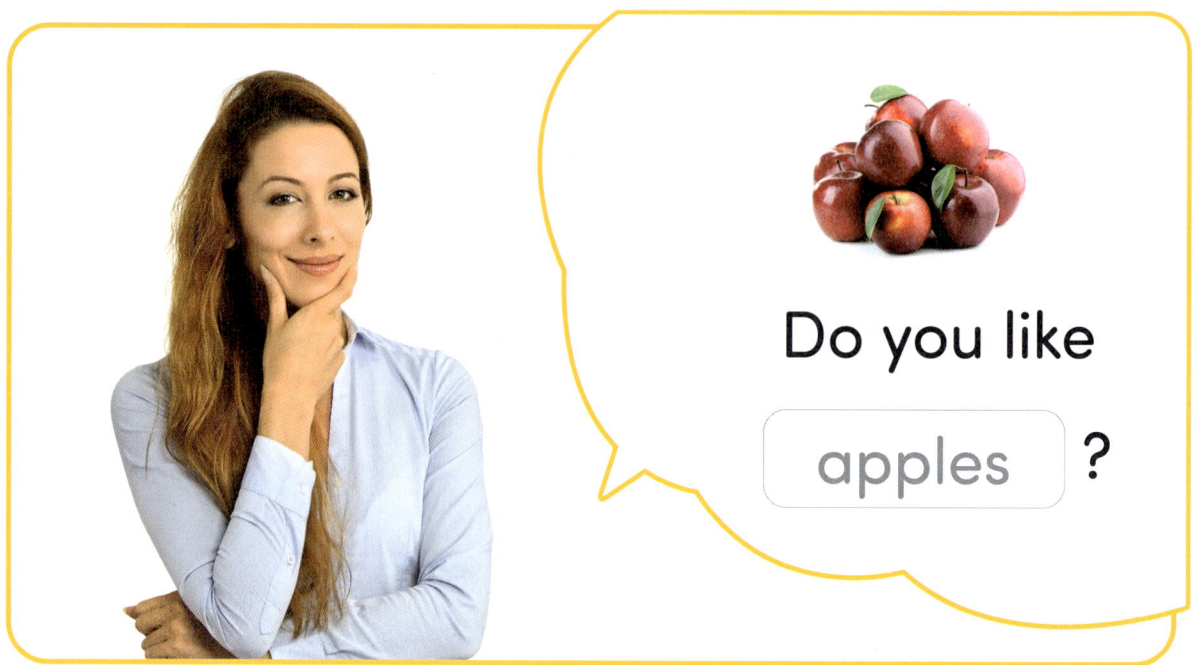

Do you like apples ?

Yes, I do.

 Ask and say.

p. 2

 p. 3 juice

 p. 5

 p. 6 apples

Sticker

 **Match.**

apples

juice

Put the food in the shopping cart.

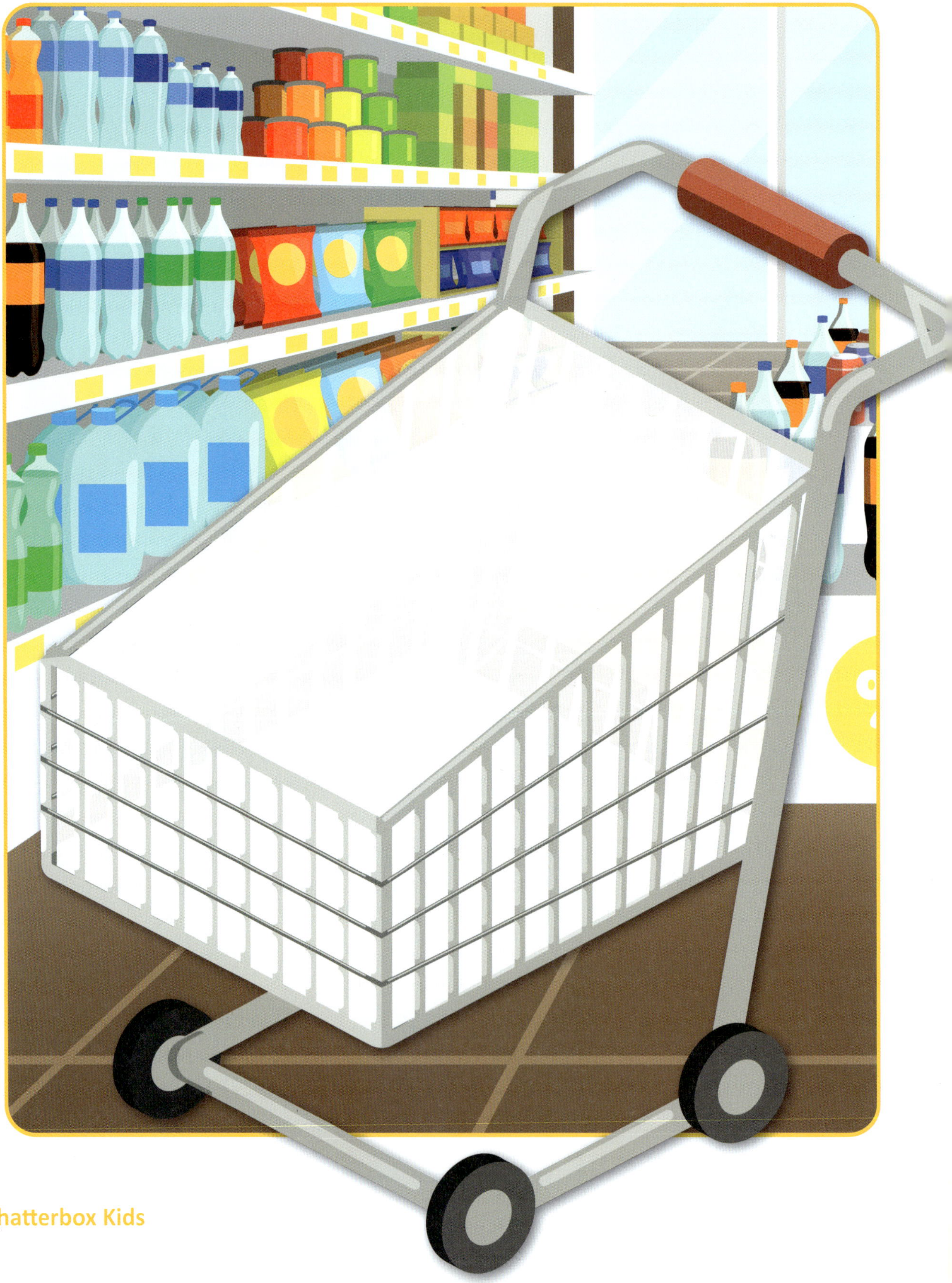

bread	apples
pizza	juice

jelly	cookies
fish	ice cream